Praise for *Tell Me About Yourself*

"Holley's book is a sage mentor between easy-to-access pages. The book contains fun and practical exercises, clever challenges, and attainable and aspirational case studies to help you build confidence and find your personal style and best self. What a joyful way to find your authentic and most confident voice!"

—**Anne Marie Burgoyne, Managing Director, Social Innovation, Emerson Collective**

"The essential field guide to owning your story. Holley does a masterful job in leading readers down a systematic path of crafting their story while keeping it real. This book is not for the faint of heart. This is about the journey of unlocking the power and potential of ourselves through our own words."

—**Vinitha Watson, founder and Executive Director, Zoo Labs**

"Holley Murchison has shown me the way to communicate who I am in a hyperconnected and extremely isolated time. In an age of polymaths and disdain for braggadocio, this book is the key."

—**Mark Brand, CEO, MB Inc./A Better Life Foundation**

"Tell me about yourself. A seemingly innocent yet challenging invitation that can send the unprepared into a fidget-ridden verbal spew of consciousness. First impressions matter, and in *Tell Me About Yourself*, Holley Murchison lays the framework for articulating the most important story you will ever tell—the story of you. This isn't your ordinary public speaking book; it's derived from thoughtful lessons Holley has learned from successfully drawing even the most apprehensive visionaries from their shell."

—**Tonya Rapley, CEO, My Fab Finance**

"In *Tell Me About Yourself*, Holley shares insights on how to step up and into one's own voice with clarity and strength. This book gracefully guides the reader through a journey of discovery while providing the space and pace needed to gather and coordinate the power that drives each individual's story."

—**Elyzabeth Holford, Founding Senior Executive, Digital Living Research Commons, Aarhus University, Denmark**

"No one has to suffer through the awkward tongue-tying and often-times confronting 'first impression.' If you are looking for a tool that gets right to the heart of the matter, *Tell Me About Yourself* is your Swiss Army knife. It is the most powerful contribution to public speaking in this era of avatars and profiles, providing readers with an analysis of self that can be shaped into a colloquial masterpiece."

—Sallomé Hralima, Executive Dream Director, The Future Project

"I have long believed that great teachers are performance coaches, and there is no better example of this than Holley Murchison. In *Tell Me About Yourself*, Holley not only helps the reader unearth his or her voice but recognizes that the leaders of the 21st century will be storytellers."

—Dave Lynn Gould, Administrator, Belin-Blank International Center for Gifted Education and Talent Development, and honors faculty, The University of Iowa

"A practical crash course in finding your inner voice and successfully communicating it. *Tell Me About Yourself* is the perfect blueprint for reinventing how you share your story and make sure the world understands who you are."

—Melissa Patenaude, Chief Experience Officer, FEWOFMANY

TELL ME ABOUT YOURSELF

TELL ME ABOUT YOURSELF

Six Steps for Accurate and Artful Self-Definition

An Action Guide
by Holley M. Murchison

Berrett–Koehler Publishers, Inc.
a BK Life book

Berrett-Koehler Publishers, Inc.
1333 Broadway, Suite 1000
Oakland, CA 94612-1921
Tel: (510) 817-2277   Fax: (510) 817-2278   www.bkconnection.com

Ordering Information

Quantity sales. Special discounts are available on quantity purchases by corporations, associations, and others. For details, contact the "Special Sales Department" at the Berrett-Koehler address above.

Individual sales. Berrett-Koehler publications are available through most bookstores. They can also be ordered directly from Berrett-Koehler: Tel: (800) 929-2929; Fax: (802) 864-7626; www.bkconnection.com

Orders for college textbook/course adoption use. Please contact Berrett-Koehler: Tel: (800) 929-2929; Fax: (802) 864-7626.

Orders by U.S. trade bookstores and wholesalers. Please contact Ingram Publisher Services, Tel: (800) 509-4887; Fax: (800) 838-1149; E-mail: customer.service@ ingrampublisherservices.com; or visit www.ingrampublisherservices.com/Ordering for details about electronic ordering.

Berrett-Koehler and the BK logo are registered trademarks of Berrett-Koehler Publishers, Inc.

Printed in the United States of America

Berrett-Koehler books are printed on long-lasting acid-free paper. When it is available, we choose paper that has been manufactured by environmentally responsible processes. These may include using trees grown in sustainable forests, incorporating recycled paper, minimizing chlorine in bleaching, or recycling the energy produced at the paper mill.

Library of Congress Cataloging-in-Publication Data

Cataloging-in-Publication Data is available at the Library of Congress.

ISBN: 978-1-5230-9466-0

22 21 20 19 18 17   10 9 8 7 6 5 4 3 2 1

Interior design and production: Dovetail Publishing Services

Cover design: Felicia Reyes, www.feliciareyesdesign.com
                and Leslie Waltzer, Crowfoot Design

Author photo: Adrian Octavius Walker

Dedication

*To you. For choosing yourself and honoring your story.
The world needs your voice now more than ever.
Thank you for taking this leap.*

*And to khoLi., Monica, Regina, Craig, and Mel—
thank you for being so down for the vision.
I couldn't have asked for a better team.*

Contents

Preface

Today you are you, that is truer than true.
There is no one alive who is youer than you.

—Dr. Seuss

Tell me about yourself

An overwhelming command, posing as a casual question—one we hear almost every day, though varying in its phrasing.

"What do you do?" asks a newcomer to your social circle.

"I'd love to hear more about your work," says a networking stranger.

"So, what can *you* do for *us*?" queries your next potential client.

"Tell me about yourself," insists your next new boss.

In any number of settings, we're frequently required to discuss ourselves, to share who we are and what we contribute to the world. Unfortunately, in most circumstances—especially, when we have just a moment's notice to respond—it can be challenging to pull all the pieces of ourselves together, conveying the perfect response, while forging a bond, sparking an idea, or advancing into deeper, more meaningful conversation.

This book is an action guide for success in all of those curious conversational moments. In it, you'll find the skills needed to accurately and artfully define yourself, as well as merge and amplify the arcs of your personal and professional journeys.

Tell Me About Yourself will challenge you to rethink the story you have been telling yourself about yourself *and* provide you with a process for not only crafting new narratives, but sharing them with authenticity, compassion, and finesse.

Enjoy the TMAY process. Share it with friends.

Here's to owning your voice.

—Holley
Founder and CEO
Oratory Glory

PS: We'd love to hear how the action guide is working for you. Share your progress and video intros on Facebook, Instagram, or Twitter (@OratoryGlory). And don't hesitate to reach out to us with your questions, breakthroughs, and feedback (hello@oratoryglory.com).

TELL ME
ABOUT
YOURSELF

Chapter 1

Why Stories Matter

Meet Holley

Twenty-seven years ago, I was just an introverted kid being tossed around the heart of New York City. As the middle child of five, in the custody of two drug-addicted-soon-to-be-separated parents, I was no stranger to the muffling of my own voice amongst my family, or in a crowd.

Actions, conversations, decisions—all of these things were happening around me, and as a six-year-old with very little agency, when it came to grown-up life topics, I was fairly practiced in opting out of all of the above.

While it's true that, early on, I often played the role of fly on the wall in most conversations, over time, I developed a knack for building genuine and meaningful connections with people through empathy and active listening in private connections. As I grew older, I began using my quiet skills to stand out in what seemed like a perpetually noisy world. Luckily, the opportunities provided to me by my stealthy behaviors also helped develop my confidence so that

I—not necessarily just my anxieties—began to challenge myself in academic and extracurricular settings. I intended to grow through my public discomfort by intentionally taking on public-facing roles, roles that demanded I be outspoken in order to succeed.

After years of playing it quiet, in third grade I picked up a basketball. I was naturally athletic and in love with the sport. It helped me have conversations and form friendships with kids in the neighborhood that I would have never approached off the court. In fourth grade, I entered my first storytelling contest (and won first place). In fifth grade, I auditioned for *The Adventures of Tom Sawyer* and earned the role of Reverend Sprague. In seventh and eighth grade, I joined the mock trial team and competed against middle school students throughout the city, learning the art of formulating and sharing a grounded, persuasive argument. In tenth grade, I became captain of both the debate and girls' basketball teams, honing my leadership, argumentation, and critical-thinking skills, while polishing a style of my own.

My college years weren't that different. I still loved basketball. I still loved finding my way to the spotlight. Fascinated and inspired by the ways words ignite things, I went on to study communications and media, specifically television and radio. I was immersed in the field, and thriving using a skill that once terrified me. And this is a version of my story—a fairly linear approximation of about 22 years of my life. But if this book serves to develop any common understanding, let it be that almost nothing about life is linear, and what little there is, is often terribly boring. And with that common understanding, let's agree that this version of my story—no matter how many times portions of it have been repeated in interviews, podcasts, or speeches—is not only a bit lulling, but also fairly inadequate. And yet, it still matters.

Meaningful moments

Take a moment to consider the greatest stories you've ever heard. Whether they're tall tales passed down at family gatherings, representations of significant figures taught in textbooks, or modes of perception created by the media, narratives agitate, educate, inspire, and motivate us by reframing some of life's most memorable and meaningful moments. Narratives help us uncover and create new truths.

That said, it's helpful to think about storytelling as a part of our social and cultural currency. Relying heavily on its market and traders, or context and audience, storytelling serves as a central barter point for entertainment and education, the preservation of culture, and the illustration and instillation of values from one party to the next. In this way, storytelling helps build and maintain community. In fact, the work of sociologist Peter L. Berger reminds us that all of what we know as human life is rooted in this cultural currency.

Stories illustrate who we are, remind us what we're capable of, highlight our uniqueness.

According to Berger, every story we share is a testament to the freedom we have to affirm. Stories illustrate who we are, remind us what we're capable of, highlight our uniqueness, and as a result, unite us or divide us in ways that shape our world. They are our declaration and purchase of our seat at the table, our place in the moment, and ultimately, in history.

So, what if we were forced to live without them?

How might our lives be different in the absence of the accounts that have defined us? How would this absence change the ways we conceptualize and understand ourselves? Without stories, how would we make sense of the layers of our experiences, beliefs, desires, dreams, values, and bodies of work? What if we weren't forced to live in the absence of accounts, but rather, the absence of accurate, artful, soul-stirring accounts? These questions bring me back to my own story.

After college, my personal journey became even more eventful, often unpredictably. In terms of my career, I went from bagging groceries at the local supermarket to preparing taxes at an accounting firm; from hosting a radio show to managing high-end construction projects at a private contracting firm; from leading volunteer projects across New York City to directing educational programming at camps and organizations around the country. Over the last 20 years, I worked over 23 jobs across the arts, education, entertainment, finance, and technology sectors—all this, before then starting two businesses of my own.

Wearing so many hats (and, honestly, doing more networking than I'd wish on anyone), I eventually grew anxious and overwhelmed whenever prompted with the infamous "So, tell me about yourself." On the one hand, I *knew* I couldn't respond with an almost two-page account of my life from elementary school to the present—no matter how transparent and linear it seemed. On the other, I was concerned that because I'd tried my hand at so many things, I would never be able to concisely express who I was professionally in conversation. This, I felt, would leave people to assume I lacked direction or focus. I worried I would be judged or misunderstood.

At times, I felt like my work history was a bit of a curse, when, in fact, there is absolutely nothing wrong or bad about exploring your curiosity and skills through different opportunities. Exploration is one of the best ways to become more aligned with our passions, path, and purpose. Accepting this as truth, I became much less focused on recounting what I or anyone else believed to be my story or life history and much more intent on accurately defining my skills, goals, and personal beliefs. I focused on articulating my path in and through the world, with my work paving the way—however winding that way might have been.

Owning our selves

Sparing us a full-blown discussion of the Jungian Self and psychology, I do want to acknowledge that the most powerful thing I've ever done has been merging my conscious desires with the professional image I had begun to create for myself in order to engage authentically as my whole self.

When I began to accept and prioritize what was unique and individual to me as a human being, I shifted. I moved from simply rehashing the events of my life to practicing the art of self-definition, which isn't so much about your life resume as opposed to *who* you are beneath the surface, as well as *how* that who informs *what* you choose to do with your time, and *where* you show up in the world. Self-definition is, simply, the articulation of how your motivations and values shape the choices and moves you make in life.

Focusing on self-definition, I even started paying closer attention to the ways people would introduce me when I shied away from doing it myself. They would never get it quite right. There was always something a little inaccurate in their telling, often an important detail that never made it into the conversation, or a summary of skills that wasn't quite inclusive or exhaustive of the work I'd done. Eventually, I vowed to take control of my story. I knew that if I wanted to make deeper connections with the people I was interacting with, I would first have to be able to clearly communicate who I was. This required a system.

First, I spent time thinking about the different conversations I might find myself having—dinner parties with investors and board members, presentations with potential clients, networking events at conferences, and other social gatherings. Then, I put together a series of questions and prompts to help me feel more prepared. Then I created a clear outline for the most critical things I wanted to share about me when describing myself, or making my own introductions. Once I had that down, I constantly practiced, preparing for any number of scenarios. And, I constantly studied, paying attention to some of my favorite communicators and storytellers, taking notes on how they defined and presented themselves. And of course, I iterated, revising my own story, and coaching others so that they could do the same.

It worked.

Today, when people ask me questions like "What do you do?" or unexpectedly invite me to introduce myself to a group of strangers, I'm no longer reluctant to say:

I'm an entrepreneur and strategist working at the intersections of communication, education, and culture. I'm motivated by and dedicated to service. I divide my time between collaborating with colleges and high schools to help them more intentionally connect students to learning pathways aligned with their passions, and developing learning experiences, special events, and coaching programs to help artists, creatives, and entrepreneurs better communicate their visions for shifting and impacting culture.

—or—

I believe in the power of marginalized voices to change the world, and believe a large part of that change lies in improving the way we learn. I'm also driven by the possibility of how much brighter our world can become if we ignite students, artists, creatives, and entrepreneurs to continue uncovering and pursuing work they love, with love. So, as an entrepreneur and communication strategist, I'm excited about finding new ways to blend my passions for education reform, culture, and the arts into projects that instigate change.

—and—

In my day-to-day work, I'm the CEO of a storytelling agency and speaker collective where I lead the development of learning experiences and curriculum and communication strategy for a number of clients. And you?

If you don't have an answer for that yet, don't worry. You will by the time you finish this book. Not only have I transcribed my proven six-step process for accurate and artful self-definition, but I've compiled profiles and case studies of some of my favorite communicators and most successful clients. As you progress through the TMAY process, remain encouraged by their examples. They all started from exactly where you are now: with themselves.

Moving forward

Introductions jump-start all of our conversations. When done well, we effectively express our core values and life's work and, in doing so, open ourselves to a variety of new connections and professional possibilities. When delivered poorly, conversations can fizzle just as quickly as they begin. Whether you're a college student, artist, entrepreneur, corporate employee, or creative professional looking to make an even deeper impact through your work, or trying to move through the ranks at your company and make meaningful contributions along the way, this book is for you.

Introductions jump-start all of our conversations.

What to expect:

Key questions, tips, and strategies for getting to the core of who you are

- An actionable six-step process to structure your responses across a range of conversations

- Case studies, interviews with, and profiles of artists, entrepreneurs, and creatives

- Practice scenarios to help you apply what you've learned throughout the book

What you'll need:

- Assorted color sticky notes (for working through activities and prompts)

- Oratory Glory storyboard (to map out your introductions)

- Your favorite pen(s) or pencil(s)—feel free to pull out all the colors!

- A journal to keep track of notes and reflections

- A smartphone or photo/video recording device (for activities and practice)

- A timer or stopwatch

- Support—The effort you put into this action guide is exactly what you'll get out of it. I encourage you to gather a crew of friends or colleagues you can rely on to hold you accountable through the process. It's definitely doable alone but even better when you have a strong group to practice alongside.

How to use this guide:

- **Take small steps.** For the sake of efficiency and accountability, each activity in the guide includes a time limit for preparation and completion. Review and complete one step at a time. If you get stuck, use the tips, strategies, and examples provided to get back on track.

- **Honor your time.** Don't attempt to breeze through the action guide in one sitting. Make sure you give yourself room to take notes, practice, bounce ideas off of friends, and reflect on possible changes.

- **Go easy on yourself.** Some of the questions may be challenging. Be patient and give yourself the space and reflection time you need to figure out the best answers for you.

- **Keep it real.** The goal is to walk away with an introduction that feels authentic to you. Don't be afraid to be vulnerable and honest with yourself along the way.

- **Show your work.** Use the storyboard on pages 34 and 35 to brainstorm and structure your responses. If you're working on multiple conversations, use one storyboard for each one. You can download your own storyboard at oratoryglory.com/TMAY-storyboard.

- **Practice.** Through the activities, you'll generate a lot of content to use in your responses. Make sure to block out time to practice your new introductions. Finding 15 to 30 minutes of practice time per week can make a world of difference.

- **Repeat.** No introduction is the same because no two conversations are the same. Apply this process to develop introductions for each of the different scenarios you face.

Chapter 2

Honing Your Voice

The warm-up

As we've established, our lives are filled with stories. And every day, each and every one of us is using these stories to build and share connections, face-to-face, through email or social media, over the phone, or via FaceTime. We use media outlets to feed stories to each other on an almost incessant basis. Some of us, for the good of many; some, for self-gain; some, unfortunately, for the detriment of others. The motivations are as infinite as the voices.

In this matrix of interconnectedness, it is increasingly necessary for each of us to not just tell a story, but understand and articulate a unique and necessary voice.

In this matrix of interconnectedness, it is increasingly necessary for each of us to not just tell a story, but understand and articulate a unique and necessary voice. Before we get started, let's gauge where you are as a storyteller and identify the type of communicator you'd like to become.

Impromptu Challenge I

Share · 5 minutes

Using the prompts below, set your timer to 2 minutes and record (audio or video) yourself telling a story about *one* of the following things:

- The best or worst group meal you've ever had,

- A fond childhood memory or defining moment, or,

- Your most memorable concert or travel experience.

Before you record, take 3 minutes to write down a few notes if you need to, but don't worry about writing out a full script. Just rely on your natural instincts and thoughts to tell the story as candidly and fully as possible.

Reflect · 10 minutes

The beauty of the previously shared memories is that we can easily recall how they made us feel. This is the same authentic approach you want to bring to your personal introductions and stories. Take 5 minutes to review what you recorded, then, using your notebook, take 5 minutes to respond to these reflection questions:

- What did you notice about your delivery, personality, and style?

- What stood out most about how you told your story?

- What was your thought process for pulling the information and story together?

- What was your favorite piece of information you shared?

- What was missing from the story that you might want to include next time?

Impromptu Challenge II

Share · 3 minutes

Pretend that you're introducing yourself to me. Using the prompts below, take 2 minutes to jot down a few important details about yourself, then set your timer to 1 minute and record yourself sharing:

- A little bit about yourself,

- Why you're using this guide, and,

- Your top one to three most challenging or frequent introduction scenarios.

- Examples: Elevator pitches, job interviews, informational meetings

Reflect · 10 minutes

Take 5 minutes to review what you recorded, then set your timer to 5 minutes and write down your reflections to the following questions:

- What stood out most about how you told your story?

- Did it differ from Impromptu Challenge I? If so, how?

- What was your thought process for pulling the information and story together?

- What picture were you trying to paint about yourself?

- Did that intention create differences between your tone or confidence in comparison to Impromptu Challenge I?

- What was missing from the story you were telling about yourself?

What if you were just as passionate and enthusiastic when making your personal introduction as you were when sharing your personal memory? Imagine the impact you could have if you spoke about your goals and passions with as much zeal as when discussing your favorite actress, musician, or even television show. Consider the kind of first impression you'd make if you lit up when speaking about your life's work in the same way you do when you hear or recall your favorite song. This is possible.

Revisiting your reflections, let's begin to think further about the differences between your two challenges. What felt good about recalling your personal memory? Does that feeling translate to any parts of your professional journey? What can you appreciate about how you represented yourself in Impromptu Challenge II? And how can you merge the best from both challenges to create an authentic and passionate framing of you and your unique contributions and desires?

We'll dive deeper into content development in the next chapter, so now is the time to really think about who you are and how you are portraying who you are through your personality and communication styles. As we move forward, keep your most difficult or frequently experienced introduction scenarios in mind. Reflect intentionally on how you might apply the above insights to frame you as an individual in those moments.

Identifying your style

[E]ach of our voices has something unique to say. Not only should I not mold my life to the demands of external conformity; I can't even find the model by which to live outside myself. I can only find it within.

—Charles Taylor, *Multiculturalism: Examining the Politics of Recognition*

When telling any story, it's important to think about the central figures involved. Who said what, when, to whom, how, and for how long? And sometimes most important, why did they say it? If we're working to tell the story of your life, even if but a brief portion of it—for instance, how you're doing today—then we must understand the central figure: you.

In order to understand you in entirety, of course, we'd need to spend a bit more time than the length of this lesson getting to know you. But consider the work we're doing together to be a process of taking distinct silhouettes, previously two-dimensional representations of you against the backdrop of categorical social settings. If this is so, then what we need to do is better understand you and your best representation in specific life moments, settings, or situations.

How are you best illuminated as a student, colleague, employee, boss, or volunteer?

How are you best illuminated as a student, colleague, employee, boss, or volunteer? What characteristic or intensity is exclusive to you?

External responses to these questions are important, yes, but more important is what you notice, attend to, and relish in yourself.

Once you identify these answers, it's important you, then, define the best way for you to embody them while engaging with others. This will serve as your ideal communication profile, or style, reminding you of how you want to communicate with others. Frequently referencing this profile will help you tailor your responses to most authentically discuss you as the central figure to any introduction.

Impromptu Challenge III

Practice · 30 minutes

Block out half an hour to write down your reflections on the questions below. Feel free to take more time, if necessary.

1. How would you describe your personality?
2. What parts of your personality do you want to stand out when you're introducing yourself to others?
3. When you're engaging different groups of people—whether in casual conversation, group work, meetings, or presentations—when are you most confident?
4. What are your communication strengths when you are introducing yourself?

5. Where do you feel you have room for improvement? Why?

6. How would you describe your ideal communication style?

7. What public figure or celebrity best represents your ideal communication style?

8. What specific communication changes (think body language, tone, volume, eye contact) would you have to make to achieve this communication style?

9. What would a stronger, more authentic introduction make possible for you in your personal, professional, or academic endeavors?

10. How willing are you to do the work to make the previously mentioned changes to your communication style?

Theo Martins

I met Theo Martins in Brooklyn, New York, in 2010 while hosting an anniversary party and music show-case for a popular blog. He was on the bill to perform that evening, and it was my first time seeing him live. Although he hailed from a city with a small town feel (Providence, Rhode Island), I remember Theo bringing big city energy to the stage that night.

From confidence to cadence to style, he engaged the crowd effortlessly, building in conversations covering everything from his obsession with video games to his love for cereal. The crowd ate it up. Theo stood out as a star—seemingly without even trying—just by making the commitment to present his full and authentic self to the audience. My favorite communicators are the ones who consistently do just that.

Today, Theo's based in Los Angeles making an even bigger splash on the West Coast than he did in New York that night. While he continues to produce and record music, he's added in a new entrepreneurial focus called Good Posture, a multimedia company housing Theo's creative endeavors in music, art, entertainment, and fashion. Through it, Theo releases limited clothing collections on his own time and his own terms, defying the conventional approach of traditional seasonal releases in fashion. He also runs a self-produced sitcom, *The Theo Show*, that airs daily on his Instagram feed.

Using traditional and social media, Theo openly shares the process of taking his ideas from inception to execution. With a "guy next door" feel and zany antics, he's identified some of the most important, entertaining parts of his life journey, and excels at communicating them casually and often, interestingly enough, with very few words.

Theo's willingness to experiment, merging both his personal and professional brands, is a reminder of just how much our life stories are ours to design, whether we're telling them online or in person. To learn more about Theo and his work, visit havegoodposture .com.

Like any other craft, storytelling requires work. And part of the work of developing compelling stories about yourself is developing the knowledge and skills it takes to discuss yourself in any moment. That means that you might have to answer these questions a few different times and in a few different ways if you're trying to plan for multiple introduction scenarios.

Like any other craft, storytelling requires work.

Consider this an independent study in self-perception, because how you perceive yourself is, most often, how you present yourself. Going forward, you'll need to frequently refer to these answers as a reminder of you as your self-constructed central figure, in addition to exactly how you want to dialogue with the world around you.

Chapter 3

Six-Step Process

I've never been convinced that experience is linear, circular, or even random. It just is. I try to put it in some kind of order to extract meaning from it, to bring meaning to it.

—Toni Cade Bambara,
Black Women Writers at Work

Here's where style meets function. TMAY's six-step storyboarding process will help you marry your situation-specific self-knowledge with the content development skills you need to create powerful introductions for any number of situations.

Use your sticky notes to keep track of your ideas (use a different color for each step). Eventually, you'll transfer them over to your storyboard. Be sure to use bullet points and phrases instead of writing in complete sentences.

You'll want to think of your introduction as the perfect appetizer. Because no one conversation (our imagined meal) is the same, the appetizer is likely to change across the different scenarios, setting the tone for what's to come.

The key to mastering the perfect intro is learning how to dissect and analyze each new scenario so that you know which intro will yield the most fruitful results.

The key to mastering the perfect intro is learning how to dissect and analyze each new scenario.

Step 1

Pick a scenario.

Go back to the three introduction scenarios you previously identified as being your most difficult or frequently occurring. Circle the one you have the most difficulty with and continue this process. You can come back to the others after you've learned how to apply the steps to this one.

Step 2

Identify your audience.

- Who are you talking to?
  + Colleagues, friends, family?

- What do they know about you so far?

- What do you know about them so far?
  + Do you have experiences or interests that overlap?

- What do you think they are interested in learning about you?
  + Why?
  + How could this new information benefit or overlap with their interests or needs?

Step 3

Clarify your response time and intent.

Given the scenario, how much time do you have to respond? Is it 30 seconds, 1 minute, 10 minutes?

Now that you've identified the timing, what's your intended outcome of this introduction? A follow-up call or meeting? An invitation to collaborate? A brief encounter that leads to a warm memory as you each go on about your lives? Too often, we enter conversations without an end goal in mind. In your imagined scenario, what do you hope comes from your introduction and the conversation it sparks?

Step 4

Reframe the question.

What question are you being asked or prompt are you being given in your chosen scenario from Step 1? Let's reframe it. What's a clearer, more coherent question that makes sense to you? From now on, anytime you're in this scenario, respond to that question instead.

Example:

If you're prompted with "Tell me about yourself" during an interview, one way to reframe the question is:

- "What can you tell me about how your personality, interests, work habits, and background will help you succeed in this position?" OR

- "What unique work experiences have brought you to this moment in time, where you're interviewing for this position?" OR

- "What educational, personal, or professional wins, passions, or aspirations that weren't highlighted in your resume make you the right fit for our team or company?"

There are four core categories of information we draw from when we tell our stories: background and interests, values and beliefs, passions and aspirations, and skills and achievements.

Step 5

Decide what you will share.

There are four core categories of information we draw from when we tell our stories: background and interests, values and beliefs, passions and aspirations, and skills and achievements. Use the questions in each of the categories below to start generating potential content for your personal introductions. Feel free to add a few of your own that are relevant to the scenarios you find yourself in.

Reflect · 30 minutes

Based on the new question you've reframed in Step 4, what are some of the key details you'd want to share in this conversation? List those details on your sticky notes, and remember to use bullet points and phrases instead of writing in complete sentences.

---

iO Tillett Wright

Sometimes we meet kindred spirits solely through shared stories and experiences. My relationship with iO Tillett Wright is the perfect example of this. I became familiar with iO through his work on MTV's *Suspect*. I remember tuning in because iO felt like the most genuine person I'd ever experienced on-screen. There was a quality about him and the way he communicated that felt familiar, welcoming, honest, even.

iO and I chatted for the first time via Twitter, in one of the most unexpected yet fruitful conversations I'd ever had. Months prior to our chat, I'd given a talk called "Eight Lessons on Love" for the CreativeMornings breakfast lecture series. iO's partner had seen my talk and made him sit down to watch it. As the story goes, iO began the talk somewhat uninterested, but by the time I'd finished giving the details of my childhood and path to self-actualization, he felt compelled to connect. Insert random Twitter DM.

In our brief exchange, iO immediately noted the parallels between our stories, upbringing, and values. We made plans to connect over lunch the next time I was in LA, but the first time I met iO was definitely not while having sweet tea and salad.

Just a few weeks after our initial chat, I received an email from Glamour magazine explaining that they wanted to feature me and five other women entrepreneurs making huge changes in the world. The photographer: iO Tillet Wright. He'd recommended me to be featured just based off of a 30-minute video and a 2-minute interaction via social media. And as grateful as I am for iO's role in landing my first full-page feature in an international magazine, I'm aware that none of this would have been possible had I not made the choice to do the work and tell one of the hardest stories about my life I've ever told, had I not chosen to bring myself— flaws and all—to the table.

But back to iO . . . after the *Glamour* shoot, we of course remained friends. And I still consider him to be one of my favorite communicators. As an artist, activist, actor, speaker, TV host, and writer, iO's work explores identity through media. And his work expands far beyond photography. Though his photos have been featured in *GQ, Elle, New York,* and the *New York Times Magazine*, iO's also a regular speaker at universities across the country, frequently sharing his personal stories with youth and working to expand what he terms our circles of normalcy.

To learn more about iO, visit darlingdays.com or follow him on Instagram at @iolovesyou.

In the next section we'll discuss strategies for how to pull the story together.

Background and Interests

- Where are you from and how has it had an impact on who you are?

- What are some of your hobbies and interests? Why do you enjoy these things?

- What's exciting in your academic or professional career? Focus on the last three years.

- List the top five adjectives that describe you. Why did you choose these?

Values and Beliefs

- What do you think about the state of the world? How do you want to help improve it?

- What character traits do your friends, family, and colleagues count on you for?

- What are the top three things that you value most? Why?

- What core beliefs do you live by? Why are these things important to you?
  + *Storyboard pro tip: List one value or core belief per sticky note.*

Passions, Dreams, and Aspirations

- What's the biggest dream you have for yourself or the world? Why?

- What are you currently doing or what have you done to get closer to achieving that dream?

- What are some of your passions and aspirations?

- How did you become interested in pursuing your passions, dreams, and aspirations?

Skills and Achievements

- What achievements are you most proud of?

- How and when did they happen?

- What skills and strengths do you bring to the table when working on teams?

- What do people count on you for most?

- How does your work contribute to the success of projects?

- How and where did you hone these skills and strengths?

- What type of work do you do now?

- How did you get there?

Step 6

Build your story.

The best responses take the setting, receiver, and the overall intention into consideration. Using the responses on your sticky notes from Steps 1 through 5 and the style-identifying activity in the previous section, start to build out your responses with the Oratory Glory storyboard provided on the next two pages.

Now that you've completed all of your steps, you can begin to transfer the information to your storyboard. Once you've transferred the information, take about 10 minutes to sit and reflect on your central figure's style paired with content. What, if any, details are repeated? How would you imagine these details brought to life using your preferred communication style?

You may not know the answers to these questions yet, which is why now is the best time to practice. You'll want to, again, use your phone or camera to record audio, video, or both. Record two to three different scenarios using varied facts from your storyboard. Record yourself telling the stories as authentically as possible, from memory. Do not write them down, unless you're creating content for a speech. And even then, do not write out full sentences; rather, jot down your most important bullet points in the order you want to relay them.

Aim to amplify what works, minimize what doesn't, and most importantly stay true to you.

As you listen or watch the recordings of yourself, jot down the most noticeable things about your presentation—good and bad. Aim to amplify what works, minimize what doesn't, and most importantly stay true to you as you practice, practice, practice.

Chapter 4

Essential Tips & Preparation

Before you start practicing your new narrative, here are a few strategies, examples, and applicable tips to keep in mind when reviewing your storyboard and fine-tuning the core elements of what you want to discuss. Since no one introduction is the same, be sure to consider how you might apply each tip to the different scenarios you highlighted in the beginning of the book.

Be clear about your aim

Every conversation has an objective. When you're sharing your story and making introductions, it's important to identify what that aim is in order to better formulate your response. Are you intending to *inform*, *persuade*, *inspire*, or *entertain* the person or people to whom you're speaking? As you reflect on your chosen scenarios, take a moment to consider what your aim is. Keep in mind that sometimes you'll have more than one.

Transfer the notes and ideas you write down to create a brief for your response.

Step 1: What's your scenario?

_____

_____

_____

Step 2: Who is your audience?

_____

_____

Step 3: How long do you have to respond, and what is the intention of the conversation?

_____

_____

Step 4: Reframe the question. What are you being asked based on your Step 1 scenario?

_____

_____

Step 5: What details do you want to share as they pertain to Step 4?

Background & Interests	Values & Beliefs	Passions, Dreams, & Aspirations	Skills & Achievements
•	•	•	•
•	•	•	•
•	•	•	•
•	•	•	•
•	•	•	•
•	•	•	•

Step 6: Build your story. Using the contents and insights from Steps 1–5, write the first draft of your new introduction in the storyboard boxes below.

Remember:

- Be clear about your aim (p. 33).
- Keep the end goal in mind (p. 36).
- Don't give it all away (p. 41).
- Take heed of the rule of three (p. 44).
- Connect the dots to weave your story together (p. 49).

You can download this storyboard template at oratoryglory.com/TMAY

For example, if you're being interviewed for a job, your intention is to inform and persuade the interviewer(s) that you are a strong candidate. So your response would be focused on articulating your history, strengths, and skills in a way that illustrates how you're the ideal person for the position.

Conversely, if you're an executive or board member who's been asked to host a fundraising event, your intention is to entertain, inform, inspire, *and* persuade the audience to keep them engaged, make sure they understand what to expect, and feel compelled to make a donation or contribution. Your introduction may include a lighthearted story about your experience and involvement with the organization or cause (*entertain/inform*), a brief rundown of the program for the evening (*inform*), and a reminder of why you've come together to celebrate and a vision of what's possible if the people in attendance continue to support the organization or cause (*inspire/persuade*).

Whatever you decide to express, a clear aim will help you clarify the most necessary information to share and filter out anything that isn't relevant to your audience or the conversation.

Keep the end goal in mind

Having an end goal is directly tied to identifying your aim. Once you're clear on the intention of your introduction, you should explore what the ideal result of the conversation would be if you were successful in achieving it. Imagine yourself in the toughest scenario you've highlighted. What are some of the possibilities and outcomes for what it could lead to? Knowing this prepares you to drive the conversation more meaningfully by asking the right questions along the way to not only share more about yourself but learn more about who you're engaging with as well.

---

*Having an end goal is directly
tied to identifying your aim.*

Now, picture yourself coming to the close of that conversation. You've introduced yourself like a pro, the dialogue progressed even better than you hoped, and you masterfully informed, persuaded, inspired, and/or entertained your audience. Consider these three questions:

- What do you want them to remember?

- How do you want them to feel?

- What do you want them to do next?

Jenna Hoge is a licensed architect based in New Jersey. As a child, she developed a love for home design and recently began exploring it more intentionally by taking on small interior design projects with family and close friends helping them to reimagine their spaces. Having worked in architecture for over 10 years, she's looking to take her passion for architecture, style, and interior design and evolve it into a side business. With a specific interest in helping couples and young professionals living in apartments maximize the way they use their space, she tells her friends and family about her new goal and asks them to refer her to people who may be interested in working with an interior designer.

At a holiday brunch, her boyfriend introduces her to a colleague who recently moved into a new apartment and is figuring out how he'd like to decorate the place. Knowing that her aim is to inform him of her expertise and persuade him that she can help, here's how Jenna might approach the three questions above:

▶ What does she want him to remember?

Though she's worked on a few small projects with friends and family, Jenna wants him to remember that her career in architecture has prepared her to manage interior design work. She also wants to communicate to him that she believes the spaces you inhabit influence your life more than you might think they do. And maybe even leave him with a few useful tips that he can apply right away.

▶ *How does she want him to feel?*

She wants him to feel impressed and moved by her passion and expertise, and that designing his home can be fun with the right support. Overall, Jenna wants him to believe she's someone with whom he should consider working.

▶ *What does she want him to do next?*

She wants him to exchange contact information with her and schedule time for a call or another in-person conversation to explore how they can work together on his design project.

Notice that Jenna's end goal isn't to seal the deal and land a new client on the spot. It's to expand on the conversation, help a potential client learn more about what he needs, and hopefully lead to a new project from there. Try not to think of your ideal outcome as the final point of transaction. It's not about what you can get from the initial connection; it's about how you can grow it.

Jenna Hoge

Here's how Jenna Hoge's new introduction shaped up after she applied the six-step process with the preparation and delivery strategies.

Her Scenario:

At a holiday brunch, Jenna's boyfriend introduces her to a colleague who recently moved into a new apartment and is figuring out how he'd like to design the place. He asks Jenna, "How did you get into interior design and what do you enjoy about it?"

Given the context, Jenna knew that she would have about one minute to respond and the end goal of the conversation was to exchange contact information to get more insight about what he needed, and explore how they could potentially work together.

Her Response:

"When I was a kid my mom and I would constantly rearrange the furniture around the house; from the living room to the dining room to our bedrooms. My mom moved the furniture, I moved the pillows. A few years after my 'rearrange-the-house' games, an amazing high school drafting teacher encouraged me to look into architecture school because of how enthusiastically I approached the class projects. Since then, architecture school and architectural practice have exposed me to a variety of designers, artists, and technologies which have informed and reinforced my love of design for the past 10 years. Still, I did not expect when I recently moved into my own apartment, and had the opportunity to design and decorate a space from scratch, how much my life would be impacted by having a home that made me happy. I was even more thrilled to see how pleased and proud the apartment made my roommates. That's what really inspired me to get into interior design; I want to get people excited about their homes by thoughtfully designing their spaces for their lives.

Don't give it all away

Have you ever been introducing yourself, feeling like things were going well, then suddenly, a shift, and you're left rambling? You began with a crystal-clear idea of what you wanted to share, but that one extra point led to an over-explanation and somewhere along the line you got tangled in the details. Or perhaps you've heard a colleague fumble on a one-minute introduction that quickly spiraled into more of a Broadway-esque mono-logue. It happens to the best of us. Sometimes we get mentally hung up on questions like—

Is this making sense?

Do they get it?

Have I said enough?

Have I said too much?

Which way is the nearest exit?

In those moments we anxiously continue talking to fill time and space in hopes that we'll ultimately be understood (or that we'll stop sweating long enough for someone to interject and save us from ourselves). It's not uncommon, but it can definitely be avoided. The mark of a really great introduction is that it entices others to ask more questions. And it's important to find the right balance of the Three Cs to get there:

Confidence

How you perceive yourself is how you present yourself. Do you believe in the story you're telling? Does it feel accurate and genuine? Is the language you're using powerful and affirming (I believe, I know, I want) or uncertain and minimizing (maybe, kind of, possibly)? When we're communicating from a place of authenticity, we're rooted in our best selves. So even in the moments when we're nervous, it's much easier to declare our truth and affirm our stories with poise. Make sure to refer back to your communication profile from the "Honing Your Voice" chapter to revisit when you're most confident.

How you perceive yourself is how you present yourself.

Clarity

Beyond tone, enunciation, and pace, having a road map for your introduction is key for clarity. It's the bridge that connects your aim to your end goal, and the buffer that keeps you from getting lost in the weeds. The preparation you've done through the storyboarding process should have given you a clear idea of where you're headed. When you're in conversation, be sure to breathe deeply, take your time, and pause when necessary to stay clear of common fillers like "um" and "uh" and to gather your thoughts if you lose your way.

Concision

As a rule of thumb, when you're thinking through the details, if you can convey them clearly and effectively in 15 words, don't use 50. What's the core information that gets your point across? Remember, the goal is to spark a broader conversation. You want to share just enough to make your audience want to connect further. Save room for more. Be the appetizer.

This tip is especially useful if you're new to a company and have to introduce yourself formally at an all-hands meeting. Or when you introduce yourself to a presenter or performer at a conference or concert. And on a more intimate level, it's great to keep in mind if you're out at dinner meeting your partner's friends for the first time.

Take heed of the rule of three

The "rule of three" is common in writing and equally applicable in oral communication. It suggests that concepts, ideas, and thoughts that are presented in threes are inherently more enjoyable, interesting, and easy to remember.

As you're introducing yourself, remember that the goal is to jump-start the conversation, not inundate people with information. So if you're feeling overwhelmed by all the different layers of your story, pause to think about what's most important for you to share and start from there.

Tiffany Hardin is an entrepreneur and strategist based in New York City. As she navigates her day-to-day life in the Big Apple, she often finds herself in spaces where she's introducing herself and her new company, Social Asset Research and Media Management (Social ARMM), to potential investors and collaborative partners. Her aim is to inform and persuade them to get involved. Having had a successful career in entertainment and talent management, her core three talking points in these conversations could be:

▶ *Her passion for art and culture, and how it led to a journey of working with top artists, influencers, entertainment executives, and Fortune 500 companies around the world.*

▶ *Hurdles she successfully navigated along the way, and insights she gained that inspired the launch of Social ARMM.*

▶ *What Social ARMM is, where it's headed, and what she's focused on now to execute the vision.*

Notice that some of Tiffany's talking points might have multiple webs of three, but they all tie back into the big picture.

If you're an entrepreneur or creative professional and want to improve the way you're introducing yourself when you have the opportunity to share more about your business, new project, or endeavor, here are some things to consider sharing:

- What are you passionate about? What type of work have you been doing to pursue that passion?

- How have those pursuits led to your current project or endeavor?

- What is your current endeavor? Provide a brief description.

- What's next? Identify a goal or project you're excited about as it relates to what you're focused on now within that project or endeavor.

Another challenging space for introductions is during conference calls with large groups of people. Though it's not always the most ideal way to communicate, whether you're updating a client or briefing a team on a new project, sometimes it's hard to avoid the infamous call with six or more people on the line who are meeting for the first time. With so many voices to acknowledge, if you're not careful, introductions can quickly begin to eat away at your meeting time. There are two key players in the conversation who can help avoid this—the person facilitating the call, and you, the participant.

As the facilitator, you're introducing yourself *and* initiating the meeting. Your core three talking points might include:

- Who you are and what role you play on the project.

- A reference to the meeting agenda, tying in the objectives and expectations for the call.

- Clear instructions and guidelines before you open the floor for participants to introduce themselves.

  + Example: "We've got an hour for our call and I want to be mindful of time. Let's begin with 30-second introductions before we move into the first item on our agenda. Grace, we'll start with you."

As a participant on the call, your goal is to be informative while keeping it short and simple enough to not disrupt the flow. Your core three talking points might include:

- Who you are and what role you play in the project.

- Why you're looking forward to being involved.

- How and why people should reach out to you throughout the project (if you're a point person).

Tiffany Hardin

Here's how Tiffany Hardin's new introduction shaped up after she applied the six-step process with the preparation and delivery strategies.

Her Scenario:

On a panel about building a career in the music industry, the moderator invites her to share more about her passion for the work she's doing and asks, "Why did you choose this path and why is the work important to you?"

Given the context, she knew that she would have about two minutes to respond and the end goal of the panel conversation was to get people excited about Social ARMM.

Her Response:

"I grew up all over the place and that was such a blessing for me because I was exposed to so many different cultures. Being culturally curious has played a big part in my career and really led me to my work in influencer marketing, partnerships, and the advertising business. My background is in the music business and talent management, is something that's always been close to my heart. Growing up, I was always in someone's talent show, in someone's musical . . . Initially, I didn't know if I wanted to be a performer, but I realized what I love most about working with talent is that you're working to fulfill a creative vision; that's something I still get to do in partnerships that I create with brands and advertisers, as well as talent. I still believe it's really important to ensure when you're working with advertisers that culture is at the forefront, so I do my best to make sure that I'm as curious as I can be so I can recommend the right cultural movements, the right cultural leaders to help facilitate and be a part of things that are happening in the marketplace."

Connect the dots to weave your story together

When introductions are disjointed and lack rhythm, they sound more like lists of character traits, accomplishments, and goals than glimpses into the window of who you are. If the intention is to stand out and make a genuine connection, you want to give people something they can follow, engage with, and hopefully relate to. Remember—you are so much more than a list or job title. Instead of leading with surface-level information or canned responses and descriptors like "I'm creative and motivated," or "I'm a leader and a team player," think of all the concrete stories and examples that highlight how you've developed qualities or skills you're proud of, and how those things have helped you grow and contribute as a person.

If you were to plant these stories and examples on a timeline, what order would you tell them in? Why?

Essentially, your introduction, or self-definition, is threading together a collection of experiences, events, and decisive moments chronicling your self-development. It also provides evidence of how you continue to show up. Revealing more than just your work and day-to-day life, your self-definition acknowledges and illuminates the construction of who you are in relation to ideas and concepts, practices, even the other human beings around you.

So remember, whether you've bumped into colleagues or classmates you haven't seen in years at a networking event, been invited to a cocktail party to meet board members and investors looking to learn more about you and what you do, or reconnected with a mentor who wants to know what you've been working on and how they can help, being able to connect the dots of your story makes a world of difference.

Practice makes perfect

We hear it all the time: the best way to improve at anything is through repeated, deliberate practice. This is no less true when it comes to introducing yourself, pitching a project, or defining your scope of work. There are a number of different approaches to practice, and I encourage you to get creative and find a routine that works best for you.

Here are a few ways to get you started:

Record yourself on audio and video

As uncomfortable as it can be to watch yourself on video or listen to the sound of your voice, no one knows your best better than you, and discomfort is where the real growth happens. In fact, I've seen the most improvement in my clients who've invested effort into recording themselves often. Start with audio before transitioning to video.

Using the times you mapped out for your scenarios in Step 3 of the TMAY process, set a timer and record at least three versions of your introduction. Practice for style and delivery, not memorization of content. With the talking points from your storyboard, try out different phrasings. Using your communication profile, critique the audio and footage based on the answers you provided to each of the questions. As you review the recordings, make note of the growth you notice in each version as well as personal feedback for how you'd like to get better.

I've found practicing with audio and video recordings incredibly helpful before community events and fundraisers, and when I'm engaging with new clients or being introduced to fellow entrepreneurs, community leaders, and advisors. For the high-stake conversations that impact personal and professional relationships, I like to be as prepared as possible.

Call on friends and colleagues and
initiate impromptu conversations
If you're working through the activities in this book with others, you've already got a built-in practice team. Pool together all of the scenarios you've outlined; work together in pairs, trios, or groups of four; time each other; and record each practice round.

If you're working through the book independently, reach out to friends and colleagues whose opinions you value and who know you well to simulate conversations with you, ask questions, and share their honest feedback to help you get better. Once your introductions begin to feel more seamless with people you know, try striking up conversation with a stranger or group of people at a networking event, coffee shop, or bar.

Use your LinkedIn profile, CV, or online portfolio

Your resumes, portfolios, and online profiles are sometimes people's first introduction to who you are. The stories you've written and told about yourself here should be in alignment with the ones you tell in person. Which is exactly what makes them a great tool for practice. If, for example, you've landed an interview for a dream project, internship, or apprenticeship, *and* you're meeting with multiple people on a team, it's important to consider more than one way of describing your experience. So when you're reviewing your LinkedIn profile, you can practice your introduction by reading the description for each endeavor you've included under your experience and telling the story of your journey through each one. Through this process, you'll find a common thread between the different opportunities you explored. This should help you separate out the best points that paint a clear picture of your passions, accomplishments, and progress.

Some questions to keep in mind as you're reviewing your profile are:

- *Which experiences are most relevant to your interview?*

- *How did you end up saying yes to the project or position?*

- *What was your role and how did you contribute?*

- *What skills, talents, or lessons did you learn while there?*

- *How could you apply those skills, talents, and lessons to this particular project or position?*

Repetition is the mother of skill. So, commit to dedicating at least 30 minutes a week to testing out your new narratives.

Repetition is the mother of skill.

Chapter 5

Show & Prove

The final sprint

You've come to the finish line (for this leg of the journey, at least)! The work doesn't end here though. In fact, in some ways, you're just getting warmed up. If you've followed along diligently, completed all the exercises, and are convinced of the importance of stories and self-definition, now comes the best part. Now, you take everything you've been exploring and developing throughout the book and share it with the community around you. After all, social responsibility starts at home, and with at least three new ways to compellingly articulate who you are, what you believe, and the value you want to add to the world, there's no better time than the present to exercise your voice in a social climate so ripe for change.

Before we dive deeper into the necessity of, and strategy for, spreading your story once you've successfully identified your core beliefs, values, and life experience, let's do a quick review of how to source your best content.

Recap

Six-step intro building process

1. Pick a scenario.

(See page 24)

In the "Honing Your Voice" chapter, you identified the top three introduction scenarios that occur most often for you. Work through each one of these based on their level of difficulty or frequency for you as you apply the next steps in the process.

2. Identify your audience.

(See pages 24–25)

Ask yourself:

- Who are you talking to?

- What do they know?

- What do you know about them to help facilitate connection and understanding?

3. Clarify your response time and intent.

(See page 25)

Given the scenario, how much time do you have to respond and what's your intended outcome? In your imagined scenario, what do you hope comes from your introduction and the conversation it sparks?

4. Reframe the question.

(See page 25)

What are you being asked? Reassess the question so that you can provide an answer that is specific and as useful as possible.

5. Decide what you will share.

(See pages 26–27)

Remember your four core categories of information:

- Background and interests

- Values and beliefs

- Passions and aspirations

- Skills and achievements

6. Build your story.

(See pages 31–32)

The best responses take the setting, receiver, and overall intention of engagement into consideration. Use the responses on your sticky notes from Steps 1 through 5 and the style-identifying activity to develop your storyboard. If you're feeling stuck, the case studies provided in this chapter will give you the direction you need.

Essential preparation and delivery tips

1. Be clear about your aim.

2. Keep the end goal in mind.

3. Don't give it all away.

4. Take heed of the rule of three.

5. Connect the dots to weave your story together.

6. Practice.

I've not only used, but taught, this process again and again. Your access to it now puts you on a level playing field with some of the most successful creatives, entrepreneurs, and corporate climbers I know. As you become more familiar with it, you'll be able to iterate on it yourself, building in and referencing your own steps or alternate resources. What you have now is a baseline; consistently incorporating other communication tools into your practice of this process will help you take your mastery of self-definition and storytelling to an entirely new level.

Going for the gold

At Oratory Glory, we believe that those who communicate confidently, compassionately, and authentically are better equipped to propel innovative ideas, excel at leadership and management, and solve complex societal challenges on a global scale.

Over the course of my career as an entrepreneur and strategist, I've been committed to uncovering and encouraging new voices in order to create cultural shifts. This has often meant moving within and throughout diverse groups (differing by access, ethnicity, gender, race, and sexuality) in order to connect and create the resources I've needed. It's also meant finding new ways to share those experiences and resources with others once the connections have been established. But I'm not the only one who's ever participated in this process. I'm able to help my clients, because I've been them. I know their stories will be able to help you all, because they've been you. At any given moment, we're all experiencing the peculiar predicament of receiving, then having to make sense of, communicate, and build around new ideas—a lot of us, doing all this with the intention of creating change.

Below, you'll find three case studies exploring the work of some of my clients who have succeeded at using the TMAY process you're learning right now. I've also added a bit about how they're using it to shift and shape the world.

Thought For Food

In 2015, just after I'd wrapped a panel about the future of storytelling at the Better World by Design conference, a recent college graduate named Jared walked over and introduced himself to me. Within the first few minutes of our conversation, he told me all about his love for travel, his passion for agriculture, and how both led to the incredible work he was doing at an equally incredible organization called Thought For Food (TFF).

He explained that Thought For Food is a global movement focused on inspiring and mobilizing students from colleges and universities around the world to develop solutions for gaining access to adequate, safe, and nutritious food—solutions for a population on track to grow to more than nine billion people by 2050.

I'm consistently drawn to collaborating with companies that are ambitious in tackling both local and global challenges. So, honestly, without much more info than that, I could have been sold. Still, I picked Jared's brain for the next 15 minutes, learning more than I imagined about Thought For Food's approach and specific goals.

I learned that TFF has a growing community of more than 8,000 students from over 600 universities in over 130 countries. They support their community through an online platform and events, offering year-round programming that includes in-person workshops, online discussions, panels, and Q&A sessions. TFF also curates tools and opportunities to help these students catalyze new ideas, launch startups, and strategically contribute to critical projects at major food security–focused organizations. On top of that, every year, TFF issues a challenge to the students in their network to form teams to participate in a global business plan competition. The top 10 finalists move on to pitch at TFF's annual summit, where they compete for a chance to take their businesses to the next level and win up to $15,000 in seed funding, bonus prizes, resources, and mentorship.

Needless to say, after my conversation with Jared, I was completely moved by TFF's mission and impact. And given the synergy between their work and Oratory Glory's commitment to catalyzing diversity by amplifying marginalized voices around the world (particularly the voices of the next generation), Jared and I were eager to explore different avenues for collaboration. A few emails, Skype calls, and a dinner meeting later, in April of 2016, I found myself in Zurich, Switzerland, in a gorgeous greenhouse that resembled a cross between *Alice in Wonderland* and *The Jungle Book*—home to the third annual Thought For Food global summit. With almost 400 people in attendance, including students, industry executives, entrepreneurs, and policy makers, I was invited to be the moderator of the two-day experience filled with keynotes, workshops, design thinking labs, and pop-up pitch rooms. I also facilitated a communication breakout session as a part of TFF's BUILD workshop track on the final day of the summit.

BUILD workshops are pop-up–style sessions led by industry experts in a variety of fields designed to help participants cultivate personal and professional skills, from productivity hacks to digital advocacy. I figured this would be the perfect space to introduce the TMAY method and focused my session on how to develop authentic introductions and leverage storytelling to make genuine connections that plant seeds for building meaningful relationships. During the session, I worked with a group of 45 emerging food system innovators, scientists, farmers, corporate leaders, venture capitalists, strategists, entrepreneurs, and students, guiding them in using the TMAY method to fine-tune their stories for introductions and conversations throughout the rest of the summit.

At the pitch competition, dinner, and wrap-up party that followed my session, I watched as they made new friendships, discussed collaborative opportunities, and confidently and authentically navigated the room as they engaged in conversation. TFF found the work we did together to be so successful that, while writing this book, I was also working with them for the second year in a row. This time, instead of just moderating and creating a breakout session, I moderated, led a live TMAY session during the summit, and coached the 10 finalist teams, leadership team, and TFF student ambassadors on how to use TMAY to better their presence and delivery. This is knowledge they'll not only be able to share with the rest of their staff, but knowledge that helps them more efficiently collaborate to solve a hugely important issue like food scarcity.

Tonya Rapley, Creator of MyFabFinance.com

Oratory Glory was my game changer. Prior to working with Holley, I didn't know how to communicate what I did without waves of anxiety compromising my message. Once I overcame my fear, we worked on tackling larger opportunities. Today I command $5,000 or more for speeches! TMAY allowed me to become more comfortable with telling MY story. . . . Working with Holley has made all the difference in my personal life and career.

—Tonya Rapley, MyFabFinance.com

I met Tonya Rapley in New York City while I was teaching a charity workshop in partnership with STOKED, a nonprofit organization using action sports and mentoring to help close the opportunity gap for middle school students. I designed the workshop for creatives and entrepreneurs launching new endeavors, and it focused on mastering the essential components of public speaking through an exploration of stories we tell about ourselves, specifically how to use TMAY in order to mine for, shape, and better structure those stories.

Tonya enrolled for support with organizing and commanding her story without anxiety compromising her message. At the time, her focus was on using her blog, MyFabFinance. com (then MyFabFICO.com), to achieve two major goals: helping millennials gain financial freedom so that they could have the flexibility to do more of what they love, and building a community of financially informed people cultivating healthy relationships with money. In line with those goals, Tonya expressed her desire to brush up on her communication and public speaking skills in order to become a leading speaker and advocate on money matters and millennial women. We worked together to deconstruct and rebuild her introduction to explain why she started MyFabFinance.com, thereby sharing her own financial journey, her passion for helping millennials take control of their finances, and her vision for growing the movement.

Since that workshop in 2013, Tonya has seen tremendous success as a result of her commitment to her communication goals. She and I continue to collaborate through one-on-one coaching and content development sessions. We've crafted signature presentations for her speaking engagements that incorporate impactful personal stories, and worked to improve her delivery, significantly reducing her nervousness and boosting her confidence through consistent practice. Tonya now tours the country speaking as a nationally recognized millennial money expert, engaging college, university, corporate, and entrepreneurial audiences on authentic leadership, crucial money lessons, and tools for building a solid financial foundation. Her website, MyFabFinance.com, is now home to an award-winning blog with content covering money, professional development, entrepreneurship, and lifestyle. There she nurtures an online community of over 50,000 people through content, courses, and challenges for becoming financially free. One challenge in particular, #BanishTheBalance, is a 60-day debt elimination challenge that has gone on to attract over 5,000 participants who've collectively paid off more than $250,000 in debt to date. Tonya also hosts and executive produces Fab Finance, a finance segment aired on Centric TV. After gracing the cover of *Black Enterprise* magazine as "The New Face of Wealth Building" in 2014, her work continues to be spotlighted in magazines, online publications, and national campaigns, including *Glamour, Marie Claire, Business Insider, Essence, Forbes*, and a national television spot for Toyota's "I Do the New" campaign.

Oberlin College & Conservatory of Music

I worked with Oberlin College & Conservatory of Music in Oberlin, Ohio, for the first time in 2016, during their annual venture accelerator, LaunchU. LaunchU is a two-week intensive boot camp and pitch competition where teams investigate everything from finance and marketing to impact analysis and the creation of a business model canvas. The experience is produced by their Creativity and Leadership department and is open to students, staff, alumni, and local Oberlin community members looking to grow ventures, including arts organizations, social impact endeavors, local businesses, and tech startups.

The department is working to build a multidisciplinary entrepreneurship program, one that challenges students to hone and explore their passions and provides them with resources to implement their ideas, tackling some of the most pressing twenty-first century challenges. Fusing pre-professional training and liberal arts, the department offers academic courses, access to funding for the development of projects, guest lectures, and various learning experiences leading up to the accelerator.

With $50,000 in investment capital up for grabs, I spent three days during LaunchU coaching 15 teams using the TMAY method in order to expand their abilities to understand, develop, and share their unique personal and business stories throughout the program and during the final pitch competition. Within that time, I watched teams completely reshape their stories with poise, sharing honest accounts of why they'd entered the program, what they wanted to accomplish through their ventures, and how they planned to do it. With renewed confidence in their vision, each team was able to find the holes in the first drafts of their pitches and fine-tune more compelling versions. Since the pitch competition, two of the three winning teams have gone on to successfully raise additional funding for their startups and are scaling their efforts to make even more impact with their growing teams.

Additionally, for the 2016–2017 school year, I rejoined Oberlin's Creativity and Leadership department as Entrepreneur-in-Residence, teaching an introductory course on entrepreneurship and leadership, and working as a part of the LaunchU leadership team to develop and roll out the next iteration of the accelerator—all while coaching the 2017 cohort on storytelling and pitch development. In the end, the LaunchU advisory board praised the 2017 cohort as the most well prepared since the first accelerator in 2012.

Outside of the accelerator, I've had the opportunity to collaborate with the college on a number of different projects through other offices and teams across campus, such as the Bonner Center for Service and Learning. At the Bonner Center, students are supported in aligning their academic, career, and extracurricular interests to engage ethically in their communities. My most recent collaboration was with the center's Bonner Scholars Program. Every year the program selects a diverse cohort of underrepresented and first-generation students to receive four-year community service scholarships. Students gain access to a number of different opportunities, such as ongoing projects with community partners, winter-term projects, and community-engaged research.

For their 2017 winter-term project, the center partnered with Paul Quinn College—a private, liberal arts, HBCU in Dallas, Texas—to send a group of 12 students to Amsterdam to learn about migration, Black diasporas, refugee experiences, and post-colonialism in the Netherlands. During the trip they'd have the opportunity to explore and network through guided tours, lectures, workshops, special events, and exhibitions. In order to help set the tone for the time students would be traveling, learning together, and making new connections abroad, I developed a workshop as part of the pre-departure program. In our session, I used the TMAY method as an entry point for students to not only understand the fundamental principles for introducing themselves, but also to effectively communicate with empathy across cultures.

Shortly after, I even trained Oberlin's Department of Rhetoric and Composition's student writing associates with TMAY; they needed to know how to extend their ability to discuss communication beyond the written page into a world of contending voices.

The students I've worked with at and through Oberlin College have been forever changed; they now have a knowledge of how to accurately articulate their vision in a world that doesn't always seek to include them or their opinions.

You're on deck

Sharing our stories empowers us to find the tribes we're meant to work with, move with purpose and agency through our lives, and catalyze change in ways that we could never accomplish alone.

Imagine how much we could soar collectively if we began to shift the focus from those who typically control the microphone in order to highlight the stories and ideas of the voices at the margins. Consider how that shift might create space for more platforms and avenues to realize, iterate, and expand the reach of viable solutions. Space where youth, women, people of color, LGBTQ communities, and all marginalized voices have a seat at the table or at the very least, feel encouraged and capable enough to pull up a chair or build a table of their own.

More than just creating an introduction to advance a conversation, this book was designed to help you feel courageous in transforming the way you discuss yourself and your work. Ultimately, it should help you define or redefine the mark you want to leave on the world. My hope is that in participating in this process and engaging in it with others, you're reminded of all that we have in common at the most human level, and how deeply connected and aligned we are beneath the surface. In addition to all the commonalities you discover,

I hope that you can more readily identify and celebrate your own unique voice, uplift and acknowledge other unique voices to claim and assert their power, and embrace that there are volumes for us to learn from one another if we open ourselves up to the possibilities. That's the big picture vision here—to continue creating and perpetuating systems of sustainable communal learning that pave the way to a more inclusive and equitable future.

Chapter 6

We Can All Win

In case you're ever feeling alone in your efforts, in case you believe yourself to be a lone voice in a disinterested world, remember that none of that is true. Generally, we're all a part of a much larger global purpose, taking shape with every action we take . . . every decision we make . . . every new, genuine connection we endeavor to foster.

In case you ever forget that, here are a few more of my past clients—people and teams just like you and yours—who are changing the world by changing how they tell their stories.

Benjamin Dyett, Cofounder of Grind

I was living in my hometown of New York City when I started teaching public speaking workshops in May of 2012. I taught my debut session at Grind, a beautiful members-only co-working space in the heart of the city, with an incredible view of Park Avenue. More than their fancy digs, I loved their focus on creating a space with more mobility and fluidity to do your best work.

After my first few workshops there, I got an email from the cofounder of the space, Benjamin Dyett. He wanted one-on-one coaching as he prepared for his first solo presentation at PSFK, an annual creative intelligence conference in New York City. With speakers and attendees working around the world in design, media, marketing, technology, and art, PSFK convenes every year to explore themes like solving complex problems through creativity and redefining the notion of social norms. Benjamin's talk was focused on the future of work and workspaces and his creation of Grind, his version of that future.

Knowing how big of an opportunity the talk would be, Benjamin wanted to improve his delivery as he shared his vision, beliefs, and work at Grind with his largest audience to date. My goal was to use TMAY to help him craft an authentic story and engage the audience with confidence and poise. With about two weeks to prepare for the conference, Benjamin and I worked together through a series of one-on-one sessions. Throughout each one, we reviewed footage from previous presentations he'd given with his cofounder to walk through areas to improve, discussed public speaking dynamics and strategies to fine-tune his delivery, developed the structure and talking points for his presentation, and video recorded practice rounds of his talk for feedback sessions. Leading up to the big day, I met up with Benjamin for the conference venue walk-through to test his presentation slides for quality and sound, and to get a sense of the stage. He went on to deliver a phenomenal talk that was very well received. Since then, Benjamin continues to speak about the future of work on panels, at conferences, and at other engagements, and Grind has since opened three new locations between New York and Chicago.

Better World by Design Conference

One of the most talented groups I've had the opportunity to work with was at the Better World by Design conference in Providence, Rhode Island. Since 2013, students from the Rhode Island School of Design and Brown University have come together annually to design an experience that celebrates interdisciplinary collaboration between designers, educators, innovators, and learners. Throughout the three-day conference, the student-led collective facilitates discussions, workshops, and panels in an effort to make design thinking more accessible and create space to apply it to ideas that can ignite positive change locally and globally.

At the 2015 conference centered on the theme of accessibility, the coordinating team focused on challenging conference-goers to address the world through the lens of design thinking, what design itself truly meant, and what it would take to make it more accessible by creating an atmosphere of "productive discomfort" they hoped would motivate attendees to collectively generate and explore solutions for making work more inclusive.

I was invited to speak on a panel about the future of storytelling and facilitate a master class on strengthening team communication for greater collective impact. The panel delved into the physical and virtual practice of storytelling; discussed how we can use it as a tool to bridge barriers across communication like language, geography, class, and cultural differences; and dissected some inherent challenges of storytelling to explore how it can become a more reliable and inclusive medium for sharing and transferring knowledge. I carried the momentum from the thoughtful questions that came up from the audience during the panel into my workshop later that afternoon.

With over 800 people attending the conference—including creative professionals, students from several different colleges and universities, entrepreneurs, and speakers disrupting their industries—I ended up with a packed room of 45 participants who eagerly made their way into my session with their hearts set on finding and owning their unique voice to better contribute to the teams and projects they were a part of. Before we began, I divided the group into teams to get better acquainted with each other and source their most challenging scenarios and communication hurdles. When each team shared what they'd uncovered, we found that they overwhelmingly struggled with similar challenges—how to present and champion ambitious ideas with confidence, how to communicate dissatisfaction, how to take accountability or give constructive feedback when things go awry, how to effectively facilitate meetings and conversations for groups, and how to make introductions that celebrated their strengths and passions without coming off as boastful.

Using the scenarios and challenges they'd sourced at the start of our workshop, I walked them through a set of strategies and practice activities for giving and receiving feedback with tact and intention, best practices to apply with ease when facilitating meetings and leading conversations, and a simple framework for selecting and ordering the most important points when presenting new ideas. I then guided them through the TMAY method, concluding the session with an opportunity for each of them to reintroduce themselves to their teams and make new connections with other teams. Each student left with boosted confidence and a tool kit for raising the bar on the impact and contributions of their work through the ways they communicated going forward.

CODE2040

Oratory Glory has been an integral partner for CODE2040's TAP Program, facilitating learning spaces for our students where they are empowered to own and tell their stories in ways that elevate their experiences and make them the foremost expert of their own narratives. Our students sometimes come from experiences that are devalued by dominant culture, and the Oratory Glory model enables them to see their own stories as beautiful and useful tools to be used for good in the world. OG's responsiveness to our programmatic needs, willingness to collaborate on workshops and curriculum, and their overall cultural competency in working in and around communities of color have made them an exemplary partner.

—Mimi Fox Melton, CODE2040

Code2040 is a San Francisco–based nonprofit that aims to close the racial wealth gap in the United States by creating pathways to educational, professional, and entrepreneurial success in the innovation economy for Black and Latinx technologists. Their bold goal is to ensure that by the year 2040---the start of the decade when the United States will be majority people of color---Black and Latinx people are proportionally represented in America's innovation economy as technologists, investors, thought leaders, and entrepreneurs.

They chip away at this goal through custom engagements, initiatives, and partnerships with tech companies committed to diversity and inclusion, and three ongoing programs tailored for top talent: their flagship Fellows Program that matches undergraduate and graduate-level students in summer internship opportunities at Bay Area, Portland, OR, and Silicon Valley companies, the Technical Applicant Prep (TAP) Program that introduces students and young professionals to the skills needed to secure internships and employment in tech companies, and the yearlong Residency Program, powered by Google for Entrepreneurs, open to emerging tech entrepreneurs in eight cities around the country.

During our collaborations together, Oratory Glory worked most closely with their TAP and Fellows Programs to facilitate tailored workshops and coaching for students. During retreats, I worked with several student cohorts, providing them with one-on-one coaching and training around the TMAY method to support them as they prepared for networking opportunities, internships, apprenticeships, and job interviews.

I also worked with the Director of Programs to customize virtual training sessions with modeled practice scenarios, strategies, activities, live Q&A, and coaching designed to help volunteers (who'd be facilitating mock interviews and coaching students) confidently share their stories and compassionately engage in one-on-one and group settings as they guided students through the standard and technical interview process.

The TAP Program also hosts Tech Trek, an all-expense-paid alternative spring break where 50 computer science majors come together in the Bay Area for a weeklong adventure of company tours and professional development workshops to network and build community to launch and sustain their careers. It concludes with an Ideathon where students work on teams to brainstorm tech solutions for social challenges. During this phase of the experience, I facilitated a pitch skills session to help students use the TMAY method to incorporate their narratives and familiarity with the problems they were addressing into the broader story of the solutions they were proposing.

In the Fellows Program, as students navigated their internships and constantly had to discuss the ins and outs of new products, I led a workshop helping them more effectively communicate technical information and ideas to nontechnical audiences through different mediums like blogs, product descriptions, and pitches. We applied the TMAY method as a framework for confidently connecting their stories in online and offline conversations as a means to pitch new ideas, share necessary information, and persuade people to take action.

Doximity

We've seen a noticeable difference in the way our Client Success team communicates with clients since working with Holley. They approach each call and meeting more prepared and with a clearer vision of the desired outcome and how to get there. We even incorporate her deck into our onboarding of new client success managers.

—Anna Millhiser, Doximity

Similar to a LinkedIn for physicians, Doximity is the fastest growing social network for doctors. Through a suite of free tools and products designed to make the world of medicine more connected and productive for doctors, they provide physicians with a secure, collaborative mobile platform for patient care solutions and alternatives, the latest in medical news, and networking.

With a community that's expanded to more than half a million physicians, nurse practitioners, and physician assistants since their 2011 launch, Doximity's client success team reached out to Oratory Glory to design a communications workshop for their growing roster of managers. Most of their client interactions occurred via email, over the phone, or on video with groups of five or more people, so I developed an empathy-based session focused on three objectives: strategies and tips to engage and inform clients with clarity and ease over webinars and during meetings, activities and exercises to speak confidently and knowledgeably when introducing them to new product features and opportunities, and frameworks and tools to effectively manage their expectations when articulating return on investment or defusing critical conversations.

Together we dissected a number of the more challenging and consistent scenarios that came up for them, such as communicating the value of products and features without technical jargon, personally persuading clients of the benefits of extending their contracts, giving and receiving feedback, and clarifying misinformation to defuse high-tension conversations. Through video-recorded practice and targeted one-on-one feedback, we were able to improvise and walk through a number of scenarios. Since our session, the hiring and client success teams have significantly improved their communication and management training processes.

General Assembly

General Assembly is a global education organization focused on teaching the most in-demand skills to passion-driven entrepreneurs, business professionals, and companies in an effort to make more strategic connections for training, staffing, and career transitions.

Since opening their doors in 2011, they've cultivated a growing community of over 35,000 graduates, 2,500 hiring partners, 250 contracted instructors, and 20 campuses worldwide. Throughout each location they offer a wide range of short-form classes and workshops, and online and immersive courses in coding, user experience and design, marketing, career development, business foundations, and data to help professionals compete in a growing technological economy.

With communication being a huge component to success in any career, from 2013 to 2016 under the business foundations and career development track, I worked with General Assembly's San Francisco campus and an instructor designing and teaching several classes and intensive weekend workshops. The overarching theme was to help new designers, engineers, developers, and other tech professionals who were often transitioning into new roles in new industries develop confidence and hone the skills necessary to confidently and authentically advocate for themselves, tell better stories, discuss their work with ease, defend their ideas, and improve their presentation skills to establish credibility and forward their careers in fast-paced, collaborative, and demanding environments. In my time on campus, I taught a roster of some of the most sought-after monthly and quarterly workshops that were often wait-listed and sold out, including one specifically dedicated to teaching the TMAY method. I worked with over 250 of some of the most talented creative professionals in the San Francisco Bay Area who made tremendous improvement as they navigated challenges like asserting themselves and standing in their power as women in the tech space, championing ideas in meetings and conversations with seasoned employees and executives, and confidently contributing their voices in spaces where they'd often been silent.

When I wasn't teaching offerings that were open to the public, I was collaborating with General Assembly's enterprise team as a facilitator. They provide customized corporate training programs and professional development opportunities with a team of vetted instructors and practitioners to US and global companies from Staples and Pearson to Condé Nast and L'Oréal, and more than 20 percent of Fortune 500 companies. Designed to help them maintain a competitive edge, support the growth and development of their teams, and continue to transform the way they do business, these trainings take place digitally, on location at partner companies, or at General Assembly's global campuses to introduce the latest skills, theories, processes, and mindsets across data and analytics, innovation culture, design, product management, digital marketing, tech, and coding to keep them ahead of the game. Working with Visa's North American and global marketing teams over a weeklong engagement, I led the storytelling component of a digital marketing immersive program with senior- and mid-level executives in communications and public relations roles. Highlighting the importance of stories and the need to continue strengthening them to inspire action across teams, I shared frameworks and strategies for gleaning and integrating insights from the data teams to maximize their impact.

Zoo Labs

When I moved to Oakland, California, in the fall of 2013, I was on the hunt for the perfect headquarters to build Oratory Glory and test out what felt like hundreds of different business development and marketing ideas floating around in my head. For the first six months I asked friends and colleagues for recommendations and shifted between my couch and different co-working spaces, but I couldn't seem to find the right fit. Then I learned about the Zoo Labs and it turned out to be exactly what I needed, with even more magic happening under the hood than I'd bargained for. The first time I toured the 8,000-square-foot state of the art facility, I knew I made the right decision. There were recording studios, multiple breakout rooms, workspaces for brainstorming and meetings, white walls galore, a private garden, and rotating galleries of local artists' work adorning the hallway walls.

Zoo Labs is home to the first music accelerator in the world. Multiple times a year, the nonprofit invites teams of musicians and bands to participate in an intensive live-in residency program focused on building a sustainable livelihood from their craft. Throughout the program, teams not only create new bodies of musical work but use the insights gathered from workshops and mentoring sessions to develop strategic plans for moving their art forward beyond the residency. On Release Day, teams close out the program by pitching their strategic plans to a carefully curated panel of wild-card guests, including music industry and tech innovators, investors, and advisors with the expertise to help implement their vision, before debuting the music they created over the course of two weeks in a live community concert open to the public. Once the residency is complete, teams have continued access to the Zoo Labs space, resources, and mentorship to bring their strategic vision to fruition.

Since 2014, I've mentored and instructed in seven residencies, speaking on storytelling and pitch panels with various experts, designing and facilitating storytelling and presentation skills workshops, and meeting one-on-one with teams using the TMAY method to help them craft their personal stories. My role in every residency has been to use communication as a vessel for guiding teams toward seeing themselves as entrepreneurs by helping them clearly articulate their journeys and progress prior to the residency, and connect those efforts to their new business approach while supporting them in developing and confidently sharing their strategic plan presentations for Release Day.

Of the teams I've had the opportunity to work closely with, some have gone on to book tours opening for nationally recognized artists, others continue to apply their art to instigate social change, and they've all found sustainable ways to communicate their brand and story in order to flourish in their careers.

By reading this book, you've become a part of a global community of thriving students, entrepreneurs, creatives, and genuinely unique groups of human beings, dedicated to using their voice to carve out a space for themselves in the world around them. You're among a group of enterprising individuals, constantly rethinking how they communicate, and how that communication is shaping the future.

My challenge to you is to make a commitment to ensure your story lives beyond the Post-it notes, cute doodles, and bullet points you've laid out on your storyboard as you navigated the six-step process. Knowing your voice has a place in the world, I'd love to help you amplify it while creating even more opportunities for you to build meaningful relationships with like-minded human beings.

My team at Oratory Glory has developed a digital platform for you to share your introductions and connect with other people like you who've invested the time, effort, and introspection this book requires. We're growing a community of some of the most talented, multidisciplinary students, artists, entrepreneurs, and creative professionals around the world; they're dedicated to bold self-expression and harnessing the power of effective communication to instigate change through their endeavors.

Visit oratoryglory.com/TMAY to learn more about how to upload your story and join them.

I hope you'll accept the challenge.

Index

About the Author

HOLLEY MURCHISON is a dreamer and a doer fueled by love and human connection whose work lies at the intersection of communication and culture. From radio hosting and youth development to project management and dream direction, to curriculum development, panel moderation, and speaking on a range of topics in entrepreneurship and leadership, Holley's last decade of work has placed her in unconventional leadership roles within, and in collaboration with, schools and companies across the arts, education, and tech industries.

As an education producer, entrepreneur, and strategist, Holley has partnered with Oberlin College, Spotify, General Assembly, Code2040, Level Playing Field Institute, and more self-employed entrepreneurs than she can count to design and curate courses and experiences ensuring the next generation has the access and knowledge they need to pursue their passions. And through her storytelling agency, Oratory Glory, she helps artists, creatives, entrepreneurs, and organizations tell stories, pitch solutions, and execute ideas that move the world forward.

She loves building with people who lead with their hearts, and working on projects that instigate change. If you're looking to connect with her, you'll most likely find her on a plane, heading to a body of water or deep and dark forest. She'll be accompanied by her partner, khoLi., and chiweenie, Cholula.

About Oratory Glory

ORATORY GLORY is a storytelling agency and speaker collective helping leaders develop intra- and interpersonal skills to communicate authentically and effectively. Committed to catalyzing diversity through the amplification of marginalized voices, we offer coaching, design learning experiences, and develop communications strategy for companies, entrepreneurial communities, and schools.

We believe that individuals who communicate confidently and authentically are better equipped to propel innovative ideas, excel at leadership and management, and solve complex societal challenges on a global scale. We also believe that those same individuals excel at sharing their learning with others. Long after engaging with Oratory Glory, our clients continue creating and perpetuating systems of sustainable communal learning.

Contact us at oratoryglory.com to explore how we can build a more radical, authentically expressed future together.

Berrett–Koehler
Publishers

Berrett-Koehler is an independent publisher dedicated to an ambitious mission: *Connecting people and ideas to create a world that works for all.*

We believe that the solutions to the world's problems will come from all of us, working at all levels: in our organizations, in our society, and in our own lives. Our BK Business books help people make their organizations more humane, democratic, diverse, and effective (we don't think there's any contradiction there). Our BK Currents books offer pathways to creating a more just, equitable, and sustainable society. Our BK Life books help people create positive change in their lives and align their personal practices with their aspirations for a better world.

All of our books are designed to bring people seeking positive change together around the ideas that empower them to see and shape the world in a new way.

And we strive to practice what we preach. At the core of our approach is Stewardship, a deep sense of responsibility to administer the company for the benefit of all of our stakeholder groups including authors, customers, employees, investors, service providers, and the communities and environment around us. Everything we do is built around this and our other key values of quality, partnership, inclusion, and sustainability.

This is why we are both a B-Corporation and a California Benefit Corporation—a certification and a for-profit legal status that require us to adhere to the highest standards for corporate, social, and environmental performance.

We are grateful to our readers, authors, and other friends of the company who consider themselves to be part of the BK Community. We hope that you, too, will join us in our mission.

A BK Life Book

BK Life books help people clarify and align their values, aspirations, and actions. Whether you want to manage your time more effectively or uncover your true purpose, these books are designed to instigate infectious positive change that starts with you. Make your mark!

To find out more, visit **www.bkconnection.com**.

Berrett–Koehler
Publishers

Connecting people and ideas
to create a world that works for all

Dear Reader,

Thank you for picking up this book and joining our worldwide community of Berrett-Koehler readers. We share ideas that bring positive change into people's lives, organizations, and society.

To welcome you, we'd like to offer you a free e-book. You can pick from among twelve of our bestselling books by entering the promotional code **BKP92E** here: http://www.bkconnection.com/welcome.

When you claim your free e-book, we'll also send you a copy of our e-newsletter, the *BK Communiqué*. Although you're free to unsubscribe, there are many benefits to sticking around. In every issue of our newsletter you'll find

- A free e-book
- Tips from famous authors
- Discounts on spotlight titles
- Hilarious insider publishing news
- A chance to win a prize for answering a riddle

Best of all, our readers tell us, "Your newsletter is the only one I actually read." So claim your gift today, and please stay in touch!

Sincerely,

Charlotte Ashlock
Steward of the BK Website

Questions? Comments? Contact me at bkcommunity@bkpub.com.

Certified

Corporation
bcorporation.net